Fermented Foods Cookbook

A Beginner's 7-Step Quick Start Guide, With Sample Probiotic Recipes

mf

copyright © 2025 Mary Golanna

All rights reserved No part of this book may be reproduced, or stored in a retrieval system, or transmitted in any form or by any means, electronic, mechanical, photocopying, recording, or otherwise, without express written permission of the publisher.

Disclaimer

By reading this disclaimer, you are accepting the terms of the disclaimer in full. If you disagree with this disclaimer, please do not read the guide.

All of the content within this guide is provided for informational and educational purposes only, and should not be accepted as independent medical or other professional advice. The author is not a doctor, physician, nurse, mental health provider, or registered nutritionist/dietician. Therefore, using and reading this guide does not establish any form of a physician-patient relationship.

Always consult with a physician or another qualified health provider with any issues or questions you might have regarding any sort of medical condition. Do not ever disregard any qualified professional medical advice or delay seeking that advice because of anything you have read in this guide. The information in this guide is not intended to be any sort of medical advice and should not be used in lieu of any medical advice by a licensed and qualified medical professional.

The information in this guide has been compiled from a variety of known sources. However, the author cannot attest to or guarantee the accuracy of each source and thus should not be held liable for any errors or omissions.

You acknowledge that the publisher of this guide will not be held liable for any loss or damage of any kind incurred as a result of this guide or the reliance on any information provided within this guide. You acknowledge and agree that you assume all risk and responsibility for any action you undertake in response to the information in this guide.

Using this guide does not guarantee any particular result (e.g., weight loss or a cure). By reading this guide, you acknowledge that there are no guarantees to any specific outcome or results you can expect.

All product names, diet plans, or names used in this guide are for identification purposes only and are the property of their respective owners. The use of these names does not imply endorsement. All other trademarks cited herein are the property of their respective owners.

Where applicable, this guide is not intended to be a substitute for the original work of this diet plan and is, at most, a supplement to the original work for this diet plan and never a direct substitute. This guide is a personal expression of the facts of that diet plan.

Where applicable, persons shown in the cover images are stock photography models and the publisher has obtained the rights to use the images through license agreements with third-party stock image companies.

Table of Contents

Introduction	7
Understanding Fermentation	9
A Brief History of Fermentation in Human Diets	9
Why Fermentation Is an Ancient Yet Modern Practice	10
What Are Fermented Foods?	12
Common Types of Fermented Foods	12
Fermentation in Different Cultures	15
Health Benefits of Fermented Foods	17
Improved Digestion	17
Enhanced Immune Function	17
Better Nutrient Absorption	18
Potential Mental Health Benefits	18
Support for Weight Management	18
Reduced Risk of Chronic Diseases	19
Improved Lactose Digestion	19
Basics of Fermentation	20
Key Ingredients Needed for Fermentation	20
Basic Equipment for Fermentation	21
How Bacteria, Yeasts, and Molds Work Together	22
Techniques for Fermenting Foods	23
Tips for Avoiding Spoilage	24
7-Step Guide to Fermentation for Beginners	**26**
Step 1: Pick Your Ingredients	26
Step 2: Gather Tools and Supplies	29
Step 3: Create the Perfect Environment	32
Step 4: Add Salt or Starter	36
Step 5: Pack and Submerge	40
Step 6: Monitor and Taste	43
Step 7: Store and Enjoy	47

Sample Recipes	**52**
Sauerkraut (Basic Cabbage Ferment)	53
Classic Kimchi	55
Pickled Carrots with Ginger	57
Fermented Jalapeño Rings	58
Garlic Dill Pickles	59
Homemade Yogurt	61
Kefir (Basic Recipe)	63
Creamy Labneh	65
Fermented Butter	66
Sourdough Bread Starter	68
Whole-Wheat Sourdough Loaf	70
Fermented Pancake Batter (Dosa or Injera)	72
Injera Batter	73
Kombucha (Basic Recipe)	75
Honey-Fermented Lemonade	77
Water Kefir	78
Homemade Beer for Beginners	80
Ginger Bug Soda	82
Fermented Hot Sauce	84
Vegan Cashew Cheese	86
Tempeh from Scratch	88
Conclusion	**90**
FAQs	**93**
References and Helpful Links	**96**

Introduction

Fermented foods hold a certain charm that's hard to ignore. They show up in cuisines across the globe, adding layers of flavor and complexity to every bite. Whether it's a jar of miso sitting on the counter or sourdough baking in the oven, fermentation embodies a mix of tradition, science, and a touch of mystery. For those who love food—or just love exploring what's possible in the kitchen—it's a subject worth digging into.

But where to begin? Fermentation can feel like a world of its own, full of jars, bubbling liquids, and strange-sounding names. It seems both endlessly fascinating and admittedly overwhelming. This guide was created to change that. It's shaped to make fermentation approachable, inviting people to step into the process—whether they're starting from scratch or simply wanting to put a name to the foods they already enjoy.

Fermented foods have a way of sparking curiosity. What makes sourdough rise without a packet of yeast? How do cucumbers turn into pickles? These questions don't just lead to answers; they open a door to creativity.

In this guide, we will talk about the following:

- Understanding Fermentation
- What are Fermented Foods?
- Health Benefits of Fermented Foods
- Basics of Fermentation
- 7-Step Guide to Fermentation for Beginners
- Sample Recipes

By the end of this guide, readers won't just know more about fermentation—they'll feel ready to take a first step, whichever way they choose. It's about discovery, inspiration, and finding small wins along the way. Whether someone dives into making their own creations or just wants to better understand what's out there, this guide opens the door wide and invites them in.

Understanding Fermentation

Fermentation is a natural process where microorganisms like bacteria, yeast, or fungi break down sugars and starches in food. This usually happens in low-oxygen environments, creating byproducts like acids, gases, or alcohols. At its core, fermentation transforms raw ingredients into something new with enhanced flavors, textures, and traits.

This process uses enzymes from microorganisms to convert carbohydrates into simpler compounds. The type of microorganism determines the result—yeast drives alcoholic fermentation for beer and wine, while lactic acid bacteria create the tangy taste in yogurt and sauerkraut.

In everyday life, fermentation is easy to spot, from the fizz in kombucha to the tang of sourdough. It's a simple yet fascinating process that nature has perfected over centuries.

A Brief History of Fermentation in Human Diets

Fermentation dates back thousands of years, born out of necessity and ingenuity. Humans began fermenting foods as early as 7,000 BCE, with examples like wine in the Caucasus and fermented milk in Mesopotamia.

For ancient cultures, fermentation was essential for preserving food before refrigeration. It allowed communities to store harvests and survive winters or food shortages. Staples like pickles, miso, and cured fish became valued for their durability and added nutrition.

Beyond survival, fermentation became part of cultural traditions. Brewing beer was a ritual in Sumerian cultures, while fermented soybeans shaped Japanese cuisine. Each region developed unique recipes based on its climate and resources.

Many of today's favorite foods—cheese, bread, and chocolate—trace their roots to ancient fermentation, showing how this method shaped the way we eat.

Why Fermentation Is an Ancient Yet Modern Practice

Fermentation has stood the test of time for good reason. What started as a practical need has evolved into a modern culinary practice that's both relevant and trendy. Its ancient roots ground it in history, while its versatility keeps it exciting today.

The recent resurgence of fermentation highlights its adaptability. Sourdough bread, kimchi, and kombucha have become everyday staples rather than niche curiosities. This revival is fueled by interest in traditional techniques, DIY food prep, and unique flavors that can't be replicated any other way.

Fermentation aligns with modern values like sustainability and reducing food waste by transforming surplus or imperfect produce into flavorful creations. It also reconnects people to slower, more mindful cooking—a refreshing change from fast, convenience-focused meals.

Simple yet sophisticated, fermentation turns basic ingredients into gourmet results. This timeless method honors tradition while inspiring innovation. From homemade pickles to five-star dishes, fermentation celebrates the past while exploring the future, proving food is both a tradition and a space for creativity.

What Are Fermented Foods?

Fermented foods are products created through the process of fermentation, where microorganisms like bacteria, yeast, or fungi break down sugars and carbohydrates in food. This natural process yields foods that are not only preserved but also enriched with probiotics, unique flavors, and improved textures.

One key feature of fermented foods is their transformation through microbial activity. For example, milk turns into yogurt when beneficial bacteria ferment its lactose into lactic acid, while cabbage becomes kimchi as it ferments into a tangy, nutrient-packed delicacy.

Common Types of Fermented Foods

Fermentation is versatile, touching almost every food group. Here's a look at some common types:

Dairy-Based Fermented Foods

Milk has long been a canvas for fermentation, resulting in creamy, tangy, and sometimes pungent outcomes. The fermentation of dairy adds probiotics, improves digestibility, and enhances flavor.

- *Yogurt*: Made by fermenting milk with bacterial cultures such as Lactobacillus bulgaricus and Streptococcus thermophilus, yogurt is a popular probiotic-rich food.
- *Cheese*: Starting with milk, different strains of bacteria or molds are used to turn it into a world of cheeses—from mild varieties like mozzarella to robust blue cheeses.
- *Kefir*: A tangy, drinkable fermented milk product rich in probiotics and enzymes, originating in the Caucasus region.

Vegetable-Based Fermented Foods

Vegetables transform through fermentation into flavorful, preserved staples packed with vitamins and probiotics.

- *Sauerkraut*: Fermented cabbage with a tangy flavor, loved in European cuisines.
- *Kimchi*: A spicy Korean dish made by fermenting vegetables like cabbage with chili, garlic, and other seasonings.
- *Pickles*: Cucumbers fermented in brine (not to be confused with vinegar-based pickles, which are not fermented).

Beverage-Based Fermented Foods

Liquid fermentation produces everything from nourishing tonics to festive spirits.

- *Kombucha*: A fermented tea made using a SCOBY (symbiotic colony of bacteria and yeast), known for its fizzy, tangy taste and health benefits.
- *Beer*: One of humanity's oldest beverages, made by fermenting grains with yeast.
- *Kvass*: A traditional Eastern European drink made by fermenting bread, offering a mildly tangy flavor.

Grain-Based Fermented Foods

Grains undergo fermentation, leading to unique textures and earthy tastes.

- *Sourdough Bread*: Made with a natural starter of wild yeast and bacteria, giving it its signature tangy flavor and chewy texture.
- *Dosa Batter*: A fermented mix of rice and lentils used in South Indian cooking to create crispy, savory pancakes.
- *Tempeh*: A fermented soy product that originates from Indonesia. Dense and nutty, it's a great plant-based protein source.

Fermentation in Different Cultures

Fermentation transcends borders, showcasing the creativity and adaptability of cultures worldwide. Here are just a few examples:

- *Korea*: Kimchi, a staple fermented vegetable dish, is made in endless variations. It's a source of national pride and nutrition.
- *Japan*: Miso (fermented soybean paste) and natto (fermented soybeans) are cornerstones of Japanese cuisine.
- *India*: Idli and dosa, made from fermented rice and lentils, are traditional dishes in South Indian households.
- *Germany*: Sauerkraut and fermented beers like lagers represent Germany's long relationship with fermentation.
- *West Africa*: Ogi, a fermented cereal porridge, is made from maize, millet, or sorghum and is a common breakfast.
- *Mexico*: Tepache, a fermented pineapple drink, showcases the ingenuity of using food scraps for delicious results.
- *Ethiopia*: Injera, a spongy sourdough flatbread made from teff flour, is a core component of Ethiopian meals.

- ***China***: Doubanjiang, a fermented paste of broad beans and chili, is a flavor powerhouse in Sichuan cuisine.

Worldwide, fermentation serves as more than just a preservation method. It tells stories about survival, resourcefulness, and celebration in every corner of the globe.

Fermented foods remind us of the brilliance of simple, natural methods. They connect us with tradition, enhance our diets, and introduce us to unique textures and tastes. By exploring and incorporating more fermented foods, we not only enrich our palates but also honor a culinary heritage that spans centuries.

Health Benefits of Fermented Foods

Fermented foods like yogurt, kimchi, sauerkraut, kefir, and kombucha have been gaining recognition for their impressive health benefits. Here's a breakdown of how they can support your health:

Improved Digestion

Fermented foods are rich in probiotics, which are beneficial bacteria that help balance the gut microbiome. These probiotics can alleviate digestive issues like bloating, constipation, and diarrhea by enhancing gut health. They also aid in breaking down nutrients, making digestion more efficient.

Enhanced Immune Function

About 70% of your immune system resides in your gut. By supporting a healthy gut microbiota, fermented foods strengthen your immune defenses. Probiotics from these foods can also stimulate the production of antibodies and improve your body's response to infections, reducing the likelihood of illness.

Better Nutrient Absorption

Fermentation enhances the bioavailability of nutrients like vitamins, minerals, and amino acids. For instance, fermented vegetables can provide more readily absorbable vitamin K2, which supports bone and cardiovascular health. This means your body can make better use of the nutrients you consume.

Potential Mental Health Benefits

The gut and brain are connected through the gut-brain axis, and a healthy gut can positively influence your mental well-being. Probiotics from fermented foods may help reduce symptoms of anxiety and depression by improving gut health. They can also boost the production of neurotransmitters like serotonin, which contributes to a better mood.

Support for Weight Management

While not universally the case, fermented foods can help maintain a healthy weight by promoting gut diversity. A well-balanced gut microbiome regulates metabolism and appetite, reducing overeating. Foods like kefir or miso are also typically low-calorie yet nutrient-dense, making them a good addition to a weight-conscious diet.

Reduced Risk of Chronic Diseases

The anti-inflammatory properties of probiotics in fermented foods may lower the risk of chronic conditions such as heart disease, diabetes, and certain cancers. The beneficial bacteria can help reduce inflammation markers in the body, creating a healthier environment overall.

Improved Lactose Digestion

For those who are lactose-sensitive, consuming fermented dairy products like yogurt or kefir can be a great alternative. The fermentation process breaks down lactose, making these products easier to digest.

By incorporating a variety of fermented foods into your diet, you can enjoy these wide-ranging health benefits while savoring their unique flavors. Always start with small amounts to ensure your gut adapts well to these probiotic-rich foods.

Basics of Fermentation

Fermentation is a fascinating technique that transforms simple ingredients into nutritious and flavorful foods, ranging from yogurt and sauerkraut to beer and kombucha. If you're new to the world of fermentation, this chapter will walk you through the key components, the science behind the process, and essential safety practices to ensure your success.

Key Ingredients Needed for Fermentation

The foundation of fermentation lies in a few simple, yet essential components. These ingredients and tools create the ideal environment for microorganisms to flourish and perform their magic.

Essential Ingredients

1. *Salt*: Salt is essential for fermentation, especially in vegetable ferments like sauerkraut or kimchi. It stops harmful microorganisms and helps beneficial bacteria thrive. Use pure, non-iodized salt for the best results.
2. *Sugar*: Sugar feeds microorganisms like yeast and bacteria. It's vital for processes like fermentation,

where yeast converts sugar into alcohol or carbon dioxide (e.g., making wine or kombucha).
3. **Water**: Clean, chlorine-free water is vital. Chlorine can inhibit the growth of necessary microbes, so you may need to use filtered or boiled-and-cooled water.
4. **Starter Cultures**: These are live microorganisms that start fermentation, like sourdough starters, kefir grains, or yogurt cultures. Some processes, like vegetable fermentation, use the natural bacteria already in the food.

Basic Equipment for Fermentation

The right equipment ensures a successful fermentation process. Some tools are essential, while others make the process more convenient or efficient.

- *Jars*: Glass jars with wide openings are ideal for fermenting foods such as pickles or kimchi. Choose jars with tight-sealing lids or fermentation-specific lids.
- *Airlocks*: Airlocks keep oxygen out of the fermenting vessel while letting gases like carbon dioxide escape. This is essential for anaerobic processes like brewing kombucha or beer.
- *Weights*: For vegetable fermentation, weights (like glass discs or food-grade ceramic stones) help keep produce submerged in brine to prevent mold growth.

- *Cheesecloth or Fermentation Lids*: For aerobic fermentation (e.g., vinegar or kombucha), breathable coverings like cheesecloth allow airflow while protecting against dust or insects.

By using the right equipment, you can create a controlled, safe environment for fermentation to occur.

How Bacteria, Yeasts, and Molds Work Together

Fermentation relies on a harmonious dance of microorganisms—each playing a unique role.

1. *Bacteria*: Lactic acid bacteria (e.g., Lactobacillus) are common in vegetable and dairy fermentation. They convert sugars into lactic acid, preserving the food and giving it tanginess.
2. *Yeast*: Yeasts such as Saccharomyces cerevisiae are vital in alcoholic fermentation, turning sugars into alcohol or carbon dioxide. They are critical for beer, bread, and wine fermentation.
3. *Mold*: Certain fermentations—like those for blue cheese or soy-based products like tempeh—rely on molds to develop unique textures and flavors.

A diverse community of microorganisms is necessary for successful fermentation. Each has its own job, and together they create a delicious end product.

Techniques for Fermenting Foods

Fermenting foods is a traditional method of food preservation that also enhances flavor and nutritional value. Here are some common techniques for fermenting foods:

1. **Lacto-Fermentation:**

    This involves using lactic acid bacteria to ferment vegetables and fruits. Common examples include sauerkraut, kimchi, and pickles. The process typically involves submerging the food in a saltwater brine to create an anaerobic environment.

2. **Alcoholic Fermentation:**

    Used in the production of alcoholic beverages like beer, wine, and cider. Yeasts convert sugars into alcohol and carbon dioxide.

3. **Acetic Acid Fermentation:**

    This process converts alcohol into acetic acid, which is used in making vinegar. It involves two stages: alcoholic fermentation followed by oxidation.

4. **Mold Fermentation:**

    Utilized in making foods like soy sauce, miso, and tempeh. Specific molds, such as Aspergillus oryzae, are used to ferment soybeans and grains.

5. **Yeast Fermentation:**

   Commonly used in baking, where yeast ferments sugars in the dough, producing carbon dioxide and causing the dough to rise.

6. **Kefir and Yogurt Fermentation:**

   Involves fermenting milk with specific bacteria and yeasts to produce kefir and yogurt, which are rich in probiotics.

Each technique requires specific conditions, such as temperature, pH, and time, to ensure successful fermentation and prevent spoilage.

Tips for Avoiding Spoilage

Fermentation is a controlled process, and it's important to take certain precautions to avoid spoilage or contamination. Here are some tips for ensuring the success of your ferments:

1. *Maintain Cleanliness*: Always start with clean jars, utensils, and surfaces. Wash your hands thoroughly to prevent introducing unwanted bacteria.
2. *Use Proper Equipment*: Opt for non-reactive containers like glass jars and avoid metals. For anaerobic fermentation, use airlocks or tight seals to keep oxygen out and prevent mold growth.
3. *Measure Ingredients Accurately*: Ensure the right salt concentration, especially in lacto-fermentation, to

create an environment that supports beneficial bacteria while deterring harmful microbes. Use filtered water if your tap water contains chlorine.
4. *Monitor Your Ferments*: Keep your fermentation environment stable at room temperature (65–75°F, or 18–24°C). Check for signs of spoilage such as foul odors, fuzzy mold, or unusual discoloration. Note that harmless surface layers, like kahm yeast, can be skimmed off.
5. *Store and Consume Safely*: Once fermentation is complete, refrigerate or store the food in a cool, dark place to slow down microbial activity and preserve the finished product.

Overall, with proper hygiene and monitoring, you can successfully ferment a variety of foods and enjoy the benefits of probiotics in your diet. Experiment with different ingredients and techniques to find what works best for you.

7-Step Guide to Fermentation for Beginners

Fermentation might sound intimidating at first, but it's actually a simple and fun process. By following these seven steps, you'll be well on your way to creating delicious fermented foods right in your own kitchen.

Step 1: Pick Your Ingredients

Choosing the right ingredients is the foundation for successful fermentation, so take your time here. Start with simple and beginner-friendly options to build confidence in the process. Here's a guide to help you make the best choices:

1. **Popular Ingredients for Beginners**

    Fermentation works well with a variety of vegetables and fruits, but some are easier to start with than others:

    - *Vegetables*: Cabbage (for sauerkraut or kimchi), cucumbers (for pickles), carrots, radishes, and saucing peppers are beginner favorites. They're

sturdy, easy to work with, and respond predictably to fermentation.
- ***Fruits***: Apples, pears, and grapes are great for beginners if you'd like to explore sweet and tangy ferments. They ferment quickly and are forgiving during the process.

If you're feeling ambitious, explore fermentation with yogurt or sourdough starters, but stick with vegetables and fruits if you want a simpler start.

2. How to Assess Freshness and Quality

The quality of your ingredients can make or break a ferment. Always look for produce that is:

- ***Fresh and crisp***: Avoid anything wilted, bruised, or showing signs of rot. Crisp, firm vegetables ferment beautifully and retain texture over time.
- ***Brightly colored and blemish-free***: Dull, soft spots or discoloration can introduce unwanted bacteria into the fermentation process.
- ***Seasonal***: Choose what's in season for the best flavor. Seasonal produce is often fresher, more flavorful, and better priced than out-of-season offerings.

Check your local farmer's market or produce section to pick items that still look vibrant and feel firm.

3. **Organic vs. Conventional Produce**

   Using organic produce isn't mandatory, but it has perks. Organic fruits and vegetables are free from synthetic chemicals that can interfere with fermentation and often have natural bacteria (like Lactobacillus) on their skins to kickstart the process. If organic isn't an option, gently wash conventional produce to remove residue.

4. **Consider Locally Sourced Ingredients**

   When possible, choose locally grown vegetables and fruits. They're typically fresher since they haven't traveled long distances, which means they stay nutrient-dense and flavorful. It's also a great way to support local farms and reduce your carbon footprint.

5. **Start Simple, Experiment Later**

   If you're new to fermentation, start with something simple like sauerkraut. Cabbage only needs salt and time, making it a great beginner project. Once you're confident, try mixed vegetable ferments, spicy kimchi, or fruit preserves with herbs and spices.

By choosing your ingredients carefully, you'll enjoy a flavorful and rewarding fermentation experience from your first batch.

Step 2: Gather Tools and Supplies

You don't need an expensive setup to start fermenting. Most of the essential tools can be found in your kitchen or easily substituted with everyday items. Here's a breakdown of what you'll need and helpful tips to make the process smoother.

1. **Essential Tools for Fermentation**

    These are the must-haves for any fermentation project. They're easy to find, inexpensive, and will help you get started on the right foot:

    - *Glass Jars*: Jars with a wide mouth are ideal for easy packing and cleaning. Mason jars in pint, quart, or half-gallon sizes work perfectly. Always pick jars that are free of chips or cracks to avoid contamination.
    - *Mixing Bowl*: Use a large bowl to mix ingredients, especially when preparing items like shredded vegetables for sauerkraut or kimchi. Stainless steel, glass, or food-safe plastic bowls all work well.
    - *Sharp Knife or Mandoline*: A good knife ensures clean, even cuts, which is important for uniform fermentation. If you're prepping lots of vegetables, a mandoline can save time and effort.

- *Wooden Spoon or Spatula*: These are great for pounding or pressing ingredients into your jar, especially for vegetable ferments that need to release juices, like cabbage. Avoid using metal spoons with acidic ferments to prevent reactions.
- *Weights*: Keeping your ingredients submerged under the brine is crucial. You can use fermentation weights (available online or at stores) or improvise with a smaller, clean glass jar or even a zip-top plastic bag filled with water.

2. **Optional Tools for Convenience**

While not necessary, these items can make your fermentation process a bit easier, especially as you experiment with more complex projects:

- *Fermentation Lids or Airlocks*: These specially designed lids allow gases to escape while preventing air and contaminants from getting in, making your process more foolproof. They're great for beginners who want to avoid the daily task of "burping" jars.
- *Vegetable Tamper or Pounder*: This wooden tool is designed for packing shredded vegetables tightly into jars and helps extract juices for brine-based ferments.

- ***Mandoline or Food Processor***: If you plan to ferment large batches, these tools save time and create consistent slices, which are ideal for uniform fermentation.

3. **Tips for Improvising with Everyday Items**

   If you don't have all the tools listed above, don't worry! You can easily substitute with items you likely already own:

   - Use clean wine or jelly bottles as weights by filling them with water and placing them inside your jar.
   - Replace fermentation lids or airlocks with plastic wrap secured with a rubber band; just remember to burp your jars daily to release gas buildup.
   - Swap special tampers with the handle of a wooden spoon to press down vegetables.

4. **How to Choose the Right Size and Type of Jars**

   The jar size depends on how much you want to ferment. For small batches, use a pint or quart jar; for larger ones, try a half-gallon jar or crock. Leave an inch or two of space at the top to prevent overflow. Glass is ideal as it doesn't absorb odors or stains and lets you monitor progress easily.

5. **Cleanliness and Safety Considerations**

   Clean tools and supplies make all the difference in preventing contamination. Here's how to ensure your workspace stays safe:

   - Wash everything—jars, bowls, knives—with warm, soapy water. Avoid using harsh chemicals or antibacterial soaps, as they can affect fermentation. Rinse thoroughly.
   - Sterilize jars if you're concerned about bacteria. Boil them for a few minutes and allow them to completely air dry before use.
   - Always start with clean hands. Handling ingredients with dirty hands can introduce unwanted microorganisms into your ferment.

By gathering these simple tools and keeping them clean, you'll create a setup that's efficient, safe, and perfect for producing delicious fermented foods.

Step 3: Create the Perfect Environment

Creating the right environment for fermentation is crucial to ensure success. A clean workspace and the right conditions allow beneficial bacteria to flourish while preventing harmful ones from taking over. Here's how to set everything up for trouble-free fermentation:

The Importance of Cleanliness

Cleanliness is the foundation of successful fermentation. While you don't need a sterile lab-like setup, it's vital to minimize the introduction of harmful microorganisms. Unwanted bacteria or debris can spoil your ferment, causing unpleasant smells, mold, or off-flavors.

How to Maintain a Clean Workspace

Start by focusing on your tools, ingredients, and workspace:

- *Wash Your Hands*: Always work with freshly cleaned hands to avoid transferring dirt or bacteria to your ingredients.
- *Clean Tools and Jars Thoroughly*: Wash all tools, bowls, jars, and weights with warm, soapy water. Rinse away any soap residues, as even mild detergent can interfere with fermentation.
- *Avoid Harsh Chemicals*: There's no need for antibacterial sprays or harsh cleaning products; they might kill off the beneficial bacteria you're trying to cultivate. Stick to plain soap and water for cleaning.
- *Wipe Down Surfaces*: Clean the countertops or any area where you'll be working. Use a mild cleaning solution like a little vinegar diluted with water if needed—just don't overdo it.

Choosing the Right Location for Fermentation

Where you place your ferment will influence the entire process. Selecting a suitable spot in your home ensures consistent results:

- ***Room Temperature***: Fermentation works best at room temperatures between 65°F and 75°F (18°C to 24°C). If it's too hot, the process might speed up and affect flavor. If it's too cold, bacteria can go dormant. If your home is too warm or cool, try adjusting the location or using tools like warm mats or cool towels.
- ***Avoid Direct Sunlight***: Keep your ferment out of direct sunlight, which can overheat the jar or degrade the beneficial bacteria over time. Choose a shady corner or inside a cupboard to maintain stable temperatures.
- ***Low Traffic Areas***: Place your jars somewhere undisturbed, like a pantry shelf or a countertop corner, where they're safe from being bumped or knocked over.
- ***Consistent Humidity Levels***: Very humid areas can promote unwanted mold growth, while extremely dry spaces might allow brine evaporation. Ensure an average humidity level that doesn't impact the jar's contents.

Monitoring Your Ferment's Environment

Fermentation is a living process, so it's essential to monitor your setup to make adjustments if needed. Here's what to keep an eye on:

- *Gas Buildup*: During fermentation, gases like carbon dioxide are released. If you're using a regular jar lid (instead of an airlock), "burp" the jar daily by quickly loosening the lid to release pressure before sealing it again.
- *Temperature Changes*: Fluctuating room temperatures can impact the process. If you notice very rapid fermentation or stalling, move the jar to a more temperature-stable spot.
- *Brine Levels*: Always ensure ingredients stay submerged under the brine. If you notice brine evaporating, add a bit of clean, salted water to maintain moisture.

Practical Tips for Beginners

- *Label Your Containers*: If you're fermenting multiple jars, note the start date, recipe, and any variations you're trying. This makes tracking your success easier.
- *Opt for a Visual Reminder*: Keep your ferment where you'll see it often, like on the kitchen counter. It'll remind you to check on progress and learn by observing the changes.

- ***Stay Patient***: Some days may seem like nothing is happening—this is normal! Trust the process and resist the urge to interfere unnecessarily.

By setting up a clean, stable environment tailored for fermentation, you'll give beneficial bacteria the best chance to do their magic. And with each ferment, you'll get better at fine-tuning this process until it becomes second nature.

Step 4: Add Salt or Starter

The addition of salt or a starter culture is a pivotal step in fermentation. These ingredients create the perfect environment for good bacteria to thrive while keeping harmful microbes in check. Here's everything you need to know to master this process.

The Role of Salt in Vegetable Ferments

Salt is essential when fermenting vegetables like sauerkraut, kimchi, or pickles. It acts as a natural preservative by drawing out moisture from the ingredients, creating a brine where good bacteria (*Lactobacillus*) can grow while harmful ones are inhibited. Salt also helps maintain the texture of vegetables, preventing them from becoming too soft or slimy.

It's important to use the right amount of salt. Too little won't create a safe environment, risking spoilage, while too much may slow down fermentation or make your end product overly salty.

How to Measure and Add Salt Correctly

For vegetable fermentation, salt is usually calculated as a percentage of the total weight of the vegetables and any water you'll use to create the brine. Here's how to get it right:

- ***General Guidelines***: A typical range is 2% to 3% salt by weight. For example, if you're fermenting 1 pound (16 ounces) of vegetables, use about 0.3 to 0.5 ounces (8 to 14 grams) of salt.
- ***Weigh Your Ingredients***: Use a kitchen scale to weigh your produce and water. This ensures accurate measurements, especially important for first-time fermenters.
- ***Mixing the Salt***: Sprinkle the measured salt evenly over your vegetables. Massage it into the produce to draw out moisture, which will naturally create the brine. For whole vegetables like cucumbers, dissolve the salt in water to make a brine before submerging the produce.

Which Salt to Use for Fermentation?

Not all salts are created equal. The type you choose can impact the quality and flavor of your ferment:

- ***Best Choices***: Pick non-iodized salt, such as sea salt, kosher salt, or pickling salt. These are free from additives that might cloud your brine or interfere with fermentation.

- ***Avoid Additives***: Stay away from iodized table salt or any salt that contains anti-caking agents, as they can disturb the fermentation process.
- ***Experiment with Flavor***: For a subtle flavor difference, you can try natural salts like Himalayan pink salt, but keep in mind this is more of a personal preference.

When to Use Starter Cultures

Starter cultures come into play for ferments like yogurt, sourdough bread, and kombucha. Unlike vegetables, which rely on naturally occurring bacteria, these ferments often need a boost to start the process. Here are some common types and how to use them:

- ***Yogurt***: Use a small amount of plain, live-culture yogurt as the starter for homemade yogurt, or purchase a powdered starter from a specialty store. You'll mix this starter with warmed milk to kickstart fermentation.
- ***Sourdough***: A sourdough starter is a mix of flour and water that captures wild yeast and lactic acid bacteria from the air. If you're just starting, you can make your own starter or acquire one from a friend or bakery. Feeding it regularly keeps it active.
- ***Kombucha***: Kombucha requires a SCOBY (Symbiotic Culture of Bacteria and Yeast) as the starter. The SCOBY floats on the surface of the tea and transforms the sweet liquid into a tangy, fizzy drink. Save some

liquid from a previous batch or get a SCOBY from a reputable source to begin.

Tips for Ensuring a Successful Ferment

- *Stick to Recipes*: Until you're more familiar with fermentation, follow reliable recipes and their salt or starter culture ratios. This ensures your first few batches stay safe and flavorful.
- *Distribute Evenly*: If using salt, take time to ensure it's evenly mixed or dissolved in the brine. Uneven salt distribution can leave parts of your ferment vulnerable to harmful bacteria.
- *Temperature Matters*: For starter cultures, follow temperature guidelines in your recipe carefully. For instance, yogurt cultures thrive in 110°F (43°C) milk, while sourdough needs room-temperature conditions.
- *Be Patient*: Whether you're salting vegetables or feeding a sourdough starter, fermentation takes time. Rushing the process can lead to inconsistent or undesirable results.

By mastering the addition of salts and starter cultures, you're creating the ideal conditions for bacteria and yeast to work their magic. With time, this step will feel intuitive, opening the door to even tastier and more creative ferments!

Step 5: Pack and Submerge

Packing and submerging your ingredients is a crucial step to ensure healthy fermentation. This process creates an oxygen-free environment where beneficial bacteria thrive while preventing mold or spoilage. Here's how to do it correctly and confidently:

Why Packing Tightly Matters

Tightly packing your ingredients in the jar serves two purposes:

- It removes air pockets, which could harbor harmful bacteria or mold. Fermentation is an anaerobic process, meaning it works best without oxygen.
- It keeps the ingredients compact, making it easier to submerge everything under the brine, which is essential for safe and consistent fermentation.

Take your time to firmly, but gently, press down the vegetables or other ingredients using clean hands, a wooden spoon, or a tamper. For example:

- When making sauerkraut, massage the cabbage to release its natural brine, and then pack it layer by layer into the jar, pressing out air as you go.
- For pickles or other whole vegetables, arrange them tightly in rows, stacking them as neatly as possible to minimize gaps.

How to Submerge Ingredients Properly

Submerging your ingredients fully in liquid is non-negotiable. If anything pokes above the brine, it could become a breeding ground for mold or yeast. Here's how to achieve the perfect submersion:

- *For Dry Brine Ferments*: Some ferments, like sauerkraut, create their own liquid when salt extracts moisture from the vegetables. Press the ingredients tightly to help release enough brine to cover them.
- *For Wet Brine Ferments*: For recipes using a pre-made brine (like pickles or carrots), pour the liquid in after packing the jar. Make sure the brine completely covers the ingredients, leaving about an inch of headspace at the top to prevent overflow as gases build up.

Using Weights to Keep Ingredients Submerged

Weights are important to stop ingredients from floating or popping above the liquid. This keeps everything safely within the brine, where the fermentation magic happens. Here are some common options for weights:

- *Store-Bought Fermentation Weights*: These glass or ceramic discs are designed to fit snugly inside jars, pressing down the contents.
- *Improvised Weights*: If you don't have fermentation-specific weights, try placing a smaller,

clean glass jar, a ramekin, or a clean rock (boiled to sanitize) inside your fermenting jar.
- *Water-Filled Bags*: A zip-top bag filled with salted water can also work as a weight. Salted water is ideal because, in case of a spill, it won't dilute the brine.

Tips for Handling Floating Ingredients

Floating pieces can be a common frustration, especially with lighter items like cabbage cores or thin slices of vegetables. Here's how to manage it:

- Use a clean piece of cabbage leaf or a food-safe silicone mat to cover the top layer of ingredients. This acts as a barrier to keep smaller, floating bits down.
- If pieces continue to float after packing, check that you've tightly pressed your ingredients and adjusted your weights as needed.

Dealing with Brine Evaporation

Sometimes, during the fermentation process, brine levels may drop. This can happen due to evaporation or absorption by the vegetables. It's important to keep an eye on this, as exposed ingredients are vulnerable to mold. Here's how to fix it:

- *Top Off with Brine*: Prepare a small batch of brine (dissolve 1 to 1.5 teaspoons of salt in 1 cup of water) and pour it in to cover any exposed areas.

- ***Recheck Your Setup***: Ensure your weights are still doing their job and that no external pressure is causing liquid to be pushed out.

By packing tightly, fully submerging your ingredients, and using clever weight solutions, you'll create the ideal environment for your ferment to flourish. These steps not only prevent common fermentation pitfalls but also boost your confidence to experiment with new ferments!

Step 6: Monitor and Taste

Monitoring and tasting your ferment is an exciting and important part of the process. This step lets you observe the transformation taking place, ensure everything is going smoothly, and decide when your ferment has reached its perfect level of flavor. Follow these tips to stay on track and enjoy the learning experience.

How to Monitor the Fermentation Process

Keeping an eye on your ferment will help you spot any potential issues early while giving you a front-row seat to the process. Here's what to watch for daily:

- ***Bubble Activity***: Fermentation produces gas as bacteria break down the sugars in your ingredients. Bubbles forming in the brine or foam at the surface are great signs that your ferment is active and healthy.

- *Sour Aroma*: A pleasantly tangy or sour smell indicates that lactic acid bacteria are hard at work. This is a good marker of progress. If you notice any foul or putrid odors, it may mean some harmful microbes have taken over—time to troubleshoot!
- *Color and Texture Changes*: Over time, you'll notice the vegetables softening slightly while their colors intensify or dull depending on the vegetable type. These changes are normal as fermentation progresses.
- *Brine Levels*: Check the brine daily to make sure it still fully covers the ingredients. If levels drop or evaporation occurs, top it off with salted water to keep your ferment safe.

The Importance of Burping Jars

For ferments sealed with an airtight lid, it's crucial to release the gases building up inside. This daily process, called "burping," prevents your jar from cracking or overflowing due to too much pressure.

- *How to Burp*: Simply loosen the jar lid for a few seconds to allow the carbon dioxide to escape, then reseal it. Be mindful of any brine that might bubble over—doing this over the sink or placing your jar on a tray can help manage potential messes.
- *Alternative Lids*: Airlock lids or specially designed fermentation lids with vents are a great option, as they

automatically release gas and reduce the need for manual burping.

Signs of Successful Fermentation

Recognizing when your ferment is progressing well—or when something's off—is key to building confidence as a fermenter. Healthy signs to watch for include:

- A steady stream of bubbles rising in the brine.
- A tangy, sour aroma that's noticeably different from when you began.
- A milky or slightly hazy brine (caused by harmless bacteria).
- A consistent taste evolution over time as the vegetables or other ingredients ferment.

How and When to Taste Your Ferment

Tasting is one of the most rewarding parts of fermentation. It's your opportunity to learn how the process changes flavors and decide when your ferment suits your palate.

- *When to Start Tasting*: Start tasting around day 3 for smaller ferments like pickles or sauerkraut, and after week 1 or 2 for larger ones. Check your recipe for timelines, but adjust based on your taste.
- *How to Taste Safely*: Use a clean utensil each time to avoid unwanted bacteria.

- *Finding the Right Flavor*: For a mild tang, stop earlier. For a stronger sourness, let it ferment longer. Taste regularly to find the perfect timing.
- *Harvesting Your Ferment*: When the flavor is right, move the jar to the fridge. Cold slows fermentation and preserves taste and texture.

Troubleshooting Common Issues

It's natural to encounter a few bumps along the way, especially if you're a beginner. Here's how to address some typical challenges:

- *Mold on the Surface*: If you see small amounts of mold on the brine, skim it off with a clean spoon. Mold happens when ingredients rise above the brine. Check your weights to keep everything submerged.
- *Brine Overflow or Pressure Build-Up*: This often happens during the early, active fermentation days. Leave enough headspace in your jar and burp regularly to prevent spills.
- *Unpleasant Smells*: Some funk is normal, but anything truly rancid may mean contamination. Discard the batch if the smell is bad and review your hygiene for the next try.

Learning from Trial and Error

Fermentation is as much an art as it is a science, and each batch you make will help you refine your skills. Here's how to get the most from the experience:

- *Take Notes*: Jot down the quantities, timing, and any observations during the process. If something goes wrong, you'll have a roadmap to troubleshoot. If it goes perfectly, you'll want to replicate it!
- *Be Curious*: Don't be afraid to experiment with different vegetables, brine levels, or fermentation times. Every tweak teaches you something new.
- *Stay Patient*: Fermentation takes time, so trust the process. Even if your first few batches aren't perfect, you're building experience and learning hands-on.

By monitoring daily, tasting actively, and troubleshooting along the way, you'll soon feel at home with the fermentation process. Each jar becomes a unique learning opportunity—and a delicious reward at the end!

Step 7: Store and Enjoy

After the time, patience, and care you've put into creating your fermented masterpiece, the final step is storing it properly and savoring the fruits of your labor. Here's how to store your ferments to extend their shelf life, maintain their delicious flavors, and make the most of them in your meals.

When Is Your Ferment Ready for Storage?

The perfect moment to transfer your ferment to cold storage depends on your taste preferences and the type of ferment. Here's how to know it's ready:

- *Taste Test*: Your ferment should have a tangy, sour flavor. For mild sourness, store it earlier. For bolder flavors, let it ferment longer.
- *Visual and Textural Clues*: Look for less bubbling, slightly softened but crunchy vegetables, and a pleasantly tangy smell. These show fermentation has slowed and it's ready to store.

Storing Your Fermented Foods

Refrigeration slows down the fermentation process significantly, preserving your creation at its peak flavor and texture. Here are some practical tips for proper storage:

- *Transfer to the Right Container*: You can store ferments in their original jar, but clean, airtight containers save fridge space and allow for smaller portions. Airtight lids prevent odors and keep ferments fresh.
- *Ensure Full Submersion*: Make sure ingredients stay covered by brine. If the brine is low, top it off with fresh salted water (1–1.5 teaspoons of salt per cup of water) to maintain a protective barrier.

- *Choose the Right Spot*: Store containers in the coldest part of your fridge, usually the back, to avoid spoilage from temperature changes.

Shelf Life and Maintenance

When stored properly, most fermented foods can last weeks, months, or even longer while continuing to develop complex flavors. Here's how to keep your ferments in great condition:

- *Consistency Is Key*: Avoid frequent temperature changes or opening the container too often, as this can introduce mold or yeast.
- *Check Regularly*: Monitor your ferments every few weeks, especially early on. If brine levels drop or you see discoloration, add more brine or remove the top layer.
- *Trust Your Senses*: Longer ferments may develop stronger flavors. Trust your nose and taste—foul smells, slimy textures, or excessive mold mean it's time to discard.

Creative Ways to Enjoy Fermented Foods

Fermented foods are as versatile as they are flavorful. Here are some delicious ways to incorporate them into your meals:

- *Side Dishes*: Serve kimchi or sauerkraut alongside grilled meats, rice bowls, or roasted vegetables for a tangy complement.

- *Snacks*: Snack directly on tangy pickles, or pair them with cheese and crackers for a fermented twist on a classic board.
- *Toppings*: Add a spoonful of fermented carrots or beets to salads, tacos, or sandwiches for a crunchy, flavorful boost.
- *Cooking Ingredient*: Stir a bit of miso paste (fermented soybeans) into soups for umami richness, or use yogurt as a base for creamy sauces and marinades.
- *Drinks*: Sip on kombucha or use it as a mixer for bright, fizzy cocktails.

Troubleshooting Storage Issues

Even after moving your ferment to the fridge, you may encounter a few issues. Here's how to handle them:

- *Brine Discoloration*: A slight change in brine color is often harmless, but cloudy or murky brine is normal for lactic acid fermentation. If it looks off or has a strong smell, discard the batch.
- *Lid Pressure Buildup*: If gas continues to build up in the jar, open it occasionally to release excess pressure, particularly in the first few weeks of refrigeration.
- *Texture Changes*: Some vegetables might soften further over time. While this is usually normal, keeping everything submerged and using airtight storage helps slow this down.

The biggest reward of fermenting at home is the satisfaction of enjoying something you've crafted from start to finish. Not only are fermented foods packed with unique flavors and gut-healthy probiotics, but they're also a testament to your growing skills as a fermenter. With each batch, you learn more about the craft, allowing you to create even more personalized and creative ferments in the future.

By following proper storage techniques and adding your personal touch to meals, you'll enjoy the fruits of your fermentation efforts for weeks or months to come. The best part? Every bite is a reminder of the care and effort you took to create something truly special!

Sample Recipes

We have put together a few sample recipes to get you started with your fermentation journey. These recipes are easy to follow and can be adapted to include ingredients of your choice.

Sauerkraut (Basic Cabbage Ferment)

Ingredients:

- 1 medium head of green cabbage (about 2 pounds)
- 1 tablespoon non-iodized salt (like sea salt or kosher salt)

Instructions:

1. Prepare the Cabbage: Peel off and set aside one outer leaf of the cabbage. Quarter the head, remove the core, and slice the cabbage into thin shreds.
2. Mix with Salt: Place the cabbage in a large bowl and sprinkle with salt. Massage the cabbage for 5–10 minutes until it softens and releases its juices.
3. Pack into the Jar: Pack the salted cabbage into a clean jar, pressing firmly with a spoon or tamper to remove air pockets. Leave about 1 inch of headspace at the top. Note that the natural brine should rise to cover the cabbage completely.
4. Add the Cabbage Leaf as a Cover: Place the reserved outer cabbage leaf on top to keep everything submerged. Add a clean weight if needed.
5. Ferment: Cover the jar with a loose lid or a fermentation lid, and leave it at room temperature (65–75°F) for 1 to 2 weeks.
6. Monitor and Taste: Check the sauerkraut daily, ensuring it stays submerged in the brine. Taste it

periodically and refrigerate once it reaches your desired tanginess.

Tips:

- Add caraway seeds, garlic, or shredded carrots for flavor variations.
- If the brine levels drop, mix 1 teaspoon of salt into 1 cup of water and top off.

Classic Kimchi

Ingredients:

- 1 medium Napa cabbage (about 2 pounds)
- 1/4 cup non-iodized salt
- 1 daikon radish, julienned
- 3 green onions, chopped
- 1/4 cup gochugaru (Korean red pepper flakes, adjust for spice preference)
- 2 tablespoons fish sauce
- 4 garlic cloves, minced
- 1 teaspoon grated ginger

Instructions:

1. Salt the Cabbage: Cut the cabbage into 2-inch pieces and place it in a large bowl. Sprinkle salt evenly between the layers and cover with water. Leave to brine for 2–4 hours, flipping occasionally. Rinse thoroughly and drain well.
2. Prepare the Paste: Combine gochugaru, fish sauce, garlic, and ginger in a small bowl to form a paste. Adjust spice levels to taste.
3. Mix with Vegetables: Add daikon radish and green onions to the cabbage. Massage the seasoning paste into the vegetables until all pieces are well coated.
4. Pack into the Jar: Tightly pack the mixture into a clean jar, leaving 1 inch of headspace. Press firmly to

remove air pockets and ensure the brine rises to cover the kimchi.
5. Ferment: Cover with a loose lid and ferment at room temperature for 3–7 days until it reaches your desired level of tanginess.
6. Store: Once fermented, store in the refrigerator.

Tips:
- For milder kimchi, reduce gochugaru or omit it entirely.
- Taste daily while fermenting and press it down to maintain submersion.

Pickled Carrots with Ginger

Ingredients:

- 4 medium carrots, peeled and cut into sticks or slices
- 1-inch piece of fresh ginger peeled and sliced
- 2 cups water
- 1 tablespoon salt

Instructions:

1. Prepare the Brine: Dissolve the salt in water to make a brine.
2. Pack the Jar: Layer the carrot sticks and ginger slices into a jar, packing them tightly. Leave 1 inch of headspace.
3. Add the Brine: Pour the brine over the carrots until they're fully submerged. Place a fermentation weight or small jar inside to keep ingredients below the brine.
4. Ferment: Cover the jar with a loose lid and leave at room temperature for 5–7 days.
5. Store: Taste daily after the first 3 days; once they reach your preferred tanginess, move the jar to the fridge.

Tips:

- Add garlic, chili flakes, or fresh herbs for extra flavor.
- If the brine evaporates, top up with additional saltwater.

Fermented Jalapeño Rings

Ingredients:

- 6–8 fresh jalapeños, sliced into rings
- 2 cups water
- 1 1/2 tablespoons salt

Instructions:

1. Prepare the Brine: Dissolve salt in water to make a brine.
2. Pack the Jalapeños: Place the sliced jalapeños in a jar, pressing down lightly to pack them tightly. Leave 1 inch of headspace.
3. Add the Brine and Weigh Down: Pour the brine over the jalapeños until they're submerged. Use a weight to keep them under the liquid.
4. Ferment: Cover loosely and leave at room temperature for 5–10 days.
5. Monitor and Store: Taste around day 5. Once the jalapeño rings have the perfect tang, transfer them to the fridge.

Tips:

- Add garlic cloves, cumin seeds, or oregano for flavor variations.
- Jalapeños may float—use a cabbage leaf or silicone mat as a barrier.

Garlic Dill Pickles

Ingredients:

- 5–6 small cucumbers (Kirby or pickling cucumbers work best)
- 3 garlic cloves, sliced
- 2 teaspoons dill seeds or 2 sprigs fresh dill
- 2 cups water
- 1 tablespoon salt

Instructions:

1. Prepare the Brine: Dissolve salt in water to create a brine.
2. Pack the Jar: Place dill seeds (or fresh sprigs) and garlic slices in the bottom of a clean jar. Add the cucumbers, packing them tightly. Leave 1 inch of headspace.
3. Pour the Brine: Add the brine to the jar until the cucumbers are fully submerged. Use a weight to ensure everything stays below the liquid.
4. Ferment: Cover loosely and leave the jar at room temperature for 5–10 days.
5. Taste and Store: Begin tasting after 5 days. Once the pickles reach the desired flavor, move them to the fridge.

Tips:

- Smaller cucumbers ferment more evenly and quickly.
- If cucumbers float, place a clean cabbage leaf or small jar on top to weigh them down.

Homemade Yogurt

Ingredients:

- 1 quart (4 cups) of whole milk (or milk of your choice)
- 2 tablespoons plain yogurt with live cultures (store-bought or from a previous batch)

Instructions:

1. Heat the Milk: Pour the milk into a pot and heat gently until it reaches 180°F (using a thermometer helps ensure accuracy). This step helps denature the proteins for better texture.
2. Cool the Milk: Remove the pot from heat and allow the milk to cool to about 110°F. This temperature is ideal for culturing yogurt.
3. Add the Starter: Scoop 2 tablespoons of yogurt into a small bowl. Add a few tablespoons of the warm milk and mix until smooth. Stir this mixture back into the pot of milk.
4. Incubate: Pour the milk into clean jars or containers. Cover them loosely and place them in a warm spot where they can maintain a temperature of around 110°F (use a yogurt maker, oven with the light on, or wrap jars in a towel). Leave to culture for 6–12 hours.
5. Taste and Chill: Check after 6 hours—if the yogurt is tangy and thickened, it's ready. Refrigerate to stop fermentation and enjoy.

Tips:

- For creamier yogurt, use whole milk or add a few tablespoons of cream.
- Adjust the tanginess by increasing or decreasing incubation time.

Kefir (Basic Recipe)

Ingredients:

- 4 cups whole milk (or any dairy/non-dairy milk you prefer)
- 1–2 tablespoons kefir grains

Instructions:

1. Combine Milk and Grains: Add kefir grains to a clean glass jar and pour the milk over them. Gently stir with a wooden or plastic spoon (avoid metal utensils).
2. Cover and Ferment: Cover the jar with a breathable cloth or coffee filter and secure it with a rubber band. Leave it at room temperature (65–75°F) for 12–24 hours.
3. Check for Readiness: Tilt the jar gently. If the milk has thickened and has a tangy aroma, the kefir is ready.
4. Strain and Store: Place a plastic strainer over another jar and pour the kefir through to catch the grains. Stir slowly to help separate the liquid. Store the finished kefir in the fridge.
5. Repeat: Add the grains to fresh milk to start the next batch.

Tips:
- For fizzy kefir, seal it in an airtight bottle for another day or two at room temperature before refrigerating.
- Adjust the fermentation time for a milder or tangier taste.

Creamy Labneh

Ingredients:

- 4 cups plain yogurt (full-fat works best)
- 1 teaspoon salt
- Olive oil (optional, for serving)

Instructions:

1. Prepare the Yogurt: Mix the yogurt and salt in a bowl until well combined.
2. Set Up the Strainer: Line a colander with cheesecloth or a clean kitchen towel and place it over a large bowl to catch the liquid.
3. Strain the Yogurt: Pour the yogurt mixture into the lined colander, fold the cloth over the top, and place in the fridge for 12–24 hours. The longer it strains, the thicker the labneh will become.
4. Transfer and Serve: Remove the labneh from the cloth and place it in a container. Drizzle with olive oil for extra flavor if desired.
5. Store: Keep labneh refrigerated for up to a week.

Tips:

- Add garlic, herbs, or spices to the strained labneh for a savory twist.
- Use the strained whey in smoothies, bread recipes, or soups.

Fermented Butter

Ingredients:

- 2 cups heavy cream (unpasteurized or pasteurized without ultra-high heat is best)
- 2 tablespoons plain yogurt with live cultures (or buttermilk with live cultures)
- Salt (optional, to taste)

Instructions:

1. Culture the Cream: Mix the heavy cream and yogurt in a clean container. Cover with a cloth and leave at room temperature for 12–24 hours, or until the cream thickens and develops a tangy aroma.
2. Churn the Butter: Pour the cultured cream into a stand mixer, food processor, or butter churn. Whip the cream until it separates into butter solids and buttermilk (takes 5–10 minutes).
3. Drain and Rinse: Strain the solids from the buttermilk. Rinse the butter under cold water, kneading it gently until the water runs clear.
4. Salt and Store: Add salt to taste (if desired) and pack the butter into an airtight container. Refrigerate and enjoy.
5. Use the Buttermilk: Save the leftover buttermilk for pancakes, biscuits, or other recipes.

Tips:

- For a more intense flavor, allow the cream mixture to culture for an additional day in the fridge before churning.
- Add finely chopped herbs or garlic to your butter for a flavored spread.

Sourdough Bread Starter

Ingredients:

- 1/2 cup whole-grain flour (like rye or whole wheat)
- 1/4 cup water (filtered, at room temperature)

Instructions:

1. Day 1 - Begin the Starter: Combine the flour and water in a clean jar or bowl. Stir until no dry flour remains, and cover loosely with a lid or clean cloth. Leave at room temperature (70–75°F) for 24 hours.
2. Day 2 - Feed the Starter: After 24 hours, discard half of the starter and add 1/2 cup all-purpose or whole-grain flour and 1/4 cup water. Stir, cover again, and leave for another 24 hours.
3. Days 3–5 - Maintain and Observe: Repeat the feeding process every 24 hours, discarding half and replenishing with fresh flour and water. By days 3–5, you should see bubbling and detect a tangy smell, indicating active fermentation.
4. Use or Store: Once your starter is lively and doubles in size after feeding, it's ready to use in recipes. If not used right away, refrigerate it and feed it weekly to maintain it.

Tips:

- Use unchlorinated water to avoid harming the natural yeasts.
- Incorporate a mix of whole-grain and all-purpose flour for a balanced starter.
- If you don't see activity by day 5, ensure the starter is kept in a warm, draft-free location and try again.

Whole-Wheat Sourdough Loaf

Ingredients:

- 1 cup active sourdough starter
- 1 1/2 cups warm water
- 3 cups whole-wheat flour
- 1 1/2 teaspoons salt

Instructions:

1. Make the Dough: Mix the sourdough starter, warm water, and flour in a large bowl until incorporated. Cover with a damp cloth and allow it to rest for 30 minutes (autolyse step).
2. Add Salt: Sprinkle the salt over the dough and knead it gently for a few minutes until the salt is evenly distributed.
3. Stretch and Fold: Over the next 3–4 hours, perform 3–4 sets of "stretch and folds" every 30–45 minutes. To stretch and fold, grab one side of the dough, stretch it upward, and fold it over itself. Repeat on all sides.
4. Bulk Ferment: Cover the dough and leave it to rise at room temperature for 4–6 hours, or overnight in the fridge, until it has doubled in size.
5. Shape the Dough: Turn the dough onto a floured surface and shape it into a tight oval or round loaf. Place it in a floured proofing basket or bowl, seam side up, and cover.

6. Final Proof: Allow the dough to proof for 1–2 hours at room temperature.
7. Bake the Loaf: Preheat your oven to 450°F with a Dutch oven inside. Carefully transfer the loaf into the hot Dutch oven, score the top with a sharp knife, cover, and bake for 20–25 minutes. Remove the lid and bake for an additional 20–25 minutes until the crust is golden brown.
8. Cool and Serve: Allow the bread to cool completely on a wire rack before slicing.

Tips:

- Use bread flour mixed with whole-wheat flour for a lighter texture if desired.
- Proof in the fridge overnight for more complex flavors.
- If you don't have a Dutch oven, use a baking stone and steam the oven by adding a pan of water.

Fermented Pancake Batter (Dosa or Injera)

Ingredients:

- 1 cup uncooked rice (like parboiled or short-grain)
- 1/2 cup split urad dal (black gram lentils)
- 1/2 teaspoon fenugreek seeds (optional)
- Water (for soaking and blending)
- Salt (to taste)

Instructions:

1. Soak the Ingredients: Rinse the rice and urad dal separately to remove excess starch. Place them in separate bowls, covering them with water. Add fenugreek seeds to the dal and soak for 6–8 hours or overnight.
2. Blend the Batter: Drain the rice and dal. Blend them separately into smooth, thick pastes. Combine the pastes in a large bowl, adding water gradually to create a pancake-like batter consistency.
3. Ferment the Batter: Cover the bowl with a loose lid or cloth and leave it to ferment in a warm spot for 8–12 hours, or until bubbly and slightly tangy. Stir and add salt to taste before using.
4. Cook Dosas: Heat a non-stick skillet or dosa pan. Pour a ladleful of batter onto the center and spread it into a thin circle. Cook on medium heat until crispy and golden. Serve with chutney or sambar.

Injera Batter

Ingredients:

- 2 cups teff flour (or a mix of teff and all-purpose flour)
- 2 cups water
- 1/4 teaspoon dry yeast (optional, for speeding up fermentation)

Instructions:

1. Mix the Batter: Combine teff flour and water in a large bowl. Stir until smooth. Add yeast if desired to jumpstart the fermentation process.
2. Ferment the Batter: Cover the bowl with a cloth and leave it at room temperature for 2–3 days, stirring daily. The batter should develop bubbles and a tangy aroma when ready.
3. Adjust Consistency: Add water as needed to create a thin, pancake-like batter.
4. Cook Injera: Use a large, non-stick skillet. Pour the batter and spread it into a thin, circular layer. Cover with a lid and cook for 1–2 minutes until the surface sets and holes form. Do not flip. Serve with stews or curries.

Tips:

- For dosa, make the batter thinner for crispier dosas or thicker for soft ones.

- For injera, teff flour provides authentic flavor, but blending with all-purpose flour can yield a softer texture.
- Fermentation times can vary with temperature, so adjust accordingly.

Kombucha (Basic Recipe)

Ingredients:

- 1-gallon water
- 1 cup sugar (preferably cane sugar)
- 6–8 black or green tea bags (or equivalent loose-leaf tea)
- 1 cup unflavored kombucha (from a previous batch or store-bought, with live cultures)
- 1 SCOBY (symbiotic culture of bacteria and yeast)

Instructions:

1. Make Sweet Tea: Boil the water and dissolve the sugar in it. Add the tea bags and steep for 5–10 minutes before removing them. Allow the tea to cool to room temperature.
2. Combine Ingredients: Pour the cooled tea into a clean, wide-mouth glass jar. Add the kombucha starter tea and gently place the SCOBY on top.
3. Ferment: Cover the jar with a breathable cloth or coffee filter and secure it with a rubber band. Leave the jar in a warm, dark, and ventilated spot (68–85°F) to ferment for 7–14 days.
4. Taste Test: After 7 days, begin tasting your kombucha daily. It's ready when it strikes a balance between tangy and sweet, according to your preference.

5. Store or Second Ferment: Transfer the kombucha to bottles and refrigerate, or move on to a second fermentation by adding flavors like fruit or spices before sealing the bottles tightly for 2–3 more days at room temperature.

Tips:

- Always use clean utensils to prevent contamination.
- A new SCOBY will usually form on top during fermentation, so use it for future batches.
- Adjust tea or sugar levels slightly to suit your taste.

Honey-Fermented Lemonade

Ingredients:

- 2 lemons, thinly sliced
- 1/4 cup raw honey
- 1 quart filtered water

Instructions:

1. Prepare the Lemons: Wash the lemons thoroughly and slice them into thin rounds. Place them into a clean jar.
2. Add Honey and Water: Pour the honey over the lemons, then add the water. Stir gently until the honey is fully dissolved.
3. Ferment: Cover the jar loosely and leave it at room temperature for 2–4 days. Stir the mixture once or twice a day to prevent mold and promote even fermentation.
4. Taste and Store: Taste the lemonade after 2 days. When it's fizzy and tangy, it's ready. Transfer the jar to the fridge to slow fermentation.
5. Serve: Pour over ice or dilute with sparkling water for extra fizz.

Tips:

- Use raw honey to ensure active beneficial microbes.
- Add a few mint leaves, ginger slices, or lavender for flavor variations.

Water Kefir

Ingredients:

- 4 cups filtered water
- 1/4 cup sugar (cane sugar is ideal)
- 1/4 cup water kefir grains
- Optional: slices of fruit, fresh herbs, or juice for flavoring

Instructions:

1. Prepare the Sugar Water: Dissolve the sugar in the filtered water completely, ensuring it's not hot, as excessive heat can harm the kefir grains.
2. Add the Kefir Grains: Place the grains into a clean glass jar and add the sugar water. Cover with a clean cloth or coffee filter secured with a rubber band.
3. Ferment: Leave the jar at room temperature in a warm spot for 24–48 hours. The longer it ferments, the less sweet and more tangy the water kefir will become.
4. Strain and Flavor: Strain the kefir grains using a non-metal strainer and transfer the liquid to another jar or bottle. Add flavors like fruit or juice if desired, and seal tightly for secondary fermentation of 1–2 days.
5. Store: Store the finished kefir in the fridge to stop fermentation and enjoy cold.

Tips:

- Avoid chlorinated water as it can inhibit the microbes.
- Save the kefir grains for endless future batches by rinsing them and storing in fresh sugar water.

Homemade Beer for Beginners

Ingredients:

- 1 gallon filtered water
- 1 pound dried malt extract (DME)
- 0.5 ounces hops (choose based on preferred flavor)
- 1 packet brewer's yeast

Instructions:

1. Boil the Wort: Heat 2 quarts of water in a large pot. Slowly stir in the malt extract until dissolved. Add the hops and boil for 45–60 minutes, stirring occasionally.
2. Cool the Wort: Remove the pot from heat and cool the mixture (called the wort) to room temperature. Use an ice bath to speed up the process.
3. Ferment: Pour the cooled wort into a clean fermentation vessel and add the remaining filtered water to make 1 gallon. Sprinkle the brewer's yeast over the top and seal with an airlock. Leave the vessel in a cool, dark place (65–70°F) for 1–2 weeks.
4. Bottle the Beer: Once the bubbling in the airlock slows to nearly zero, siphon the beer into clean bottles and seal with caps. Allow the beer to carbonate at room temperature for another 1–2 weeks.
5. Chill and Enjoy: Refrigerate your homemade beer for a few days before serving.

Tips:

- Sanitize all tools to avoid contamination.
- Experiment with different hops or add flavors like orange peel or coriander.

Ginger Bug Soda

Ingredients:

- 2 cups water (filtered)
- 2 teaspoons grated fresh ginger (with skin)
- 2 teaspoons sugar (cane sugar is best)
- For soda base: 4 cups water, 1/4 cup sugar, and juice or herbal tea of your choice

Instructions:

1. Make the Ginger Bug: Combine water, grated ginger, and sugar in a jar. Stir to dissolve. Cover with a cloth secured with a band and leave at room temperature.
2. Feed Daily: Each day, add 1 teaspoon of sugar and 1 teaspoon of grated ginger, stirring well. After 3–7 days, the ginger bug will become bubbly and ready to use.
3. Prepare the Soda Base: Boil water and dissolve 1/4 cup sugar for the soda base. Allow it to cool to room temperature, then combine it with juice or tea of your choice.
4. Ferment the Soda: Add 1/4 cup of ginger bug liquid to the soda base and transfer it to bottles. Seal tightly and leave at room temperature to carbonate for 1–3 days.
5. Chill and Serve: Once bubbly, refrigerate the bottles and enjoy chilled.

Tips:

- Test for carbonation daily by carefully opening the bottle.
- Replace ginger bug feedings when some liquid is removed for soda.

Fermented Hot Sauce

Ingredients:

- 1 pound fresh chili peppers (e.g., jalapeño, habanero, or a mix)
- 4–6 garlic cloves (optional)
- 2 teaspoons non-iodized salt
- 2 cups filtered water (or enough to cover the peppers)

Instructions:

1. Prepare the Peppers: Wash the chili peppers and slice them into halves or quarters. You can remove seeds for a milder sauce or keep them for extra heat. Peel and slice the garlic if using.
2. Mix the Brine: Dissolve the salt in filtered water to create the brine.
3. Pack the Jar: Tightly pack the peppers and garlic into a clean glass jar, leaving about 1–2 inches of space at the top. Pour the brine over the peppers until fully submerged. Use a fermentation weight or a clean leaf of cabbage to keep everything below the brine.
4. Ferment: Cover the jar with a breathable cloth or fermentation lid. Place it in a cool, dark spot for 5–14 days. Bubbles and a sour aroma will signal active fermentation.
5. Blend and Store: Once fermented to your liking, transfer the peppers and a bit of the brine to a blender.

Blend until smooth, adding more brine for a thinner consistency. Pour into bottles and refrigerate.
6. Serve: Use the hot sauce as a spicy condiment for any dish!

Tips:

- Taste your ferment every few days to determine when it's tangy enough.
- Add carrots or fruity peppers for a sweet twist.
- For longer storage, strain the pulp from the liquid and boil the hot sauce before bottling.

Vegan Cashew Cheese

Ingredients:

- 2 cups raw cashews, soaked for 4–6 hours
- 1/4 cup water (plus more if needed)
- 1–2 tablespoons lemon juice
- 1–2 tablespoons unflavored non-dairy yogurt or water kefir (for fermentation)
- 1 teaspoon salt (optional)
- Nutritional yeast (optional, for cheesy flavor)

Instructions:

1. Prepare the Cashews: Drain and rinse the soaked cashews thoroughly.
2. Blend: Add the cashews, water, lemon juice, yogurt/kefir, and salt to a high-speed blender or food processor. Blend until smooth, scraping down the sides as needed. Add more water if needed to reach a creamy consistency.
3. Ferment: Transfer the cashew mixture to a clean glass or ceramic bowl. Cover loosely with a cloth or compostable wrap and leave it at room temperature for 12–24 hours. The tangy flavor will develop as it ferments.
4. Adjust Flavors: Taste the fermented cheese and adjust with more salt, lemon juice, or nutritional yeast as desired.

5. Serve or Store: Use immediately as a spread or refrigerate in an airtight container for up to a week.

Tips:

- For a firmer cheese, press the mixture into a mold and refrigerate.
- Add garlic, herbs, or smoked paprika for extra flavor.
- If the cheese smells unpleasant or mold develops, discard it and try again with thoroughly sanitized tools.

Tempeh from Scratch

Ingredients:

- 1 cup dried soybeans
- 1 tablespoon vinegar (e.g., apple cider or white vinegar)
- 1 teaspoon tempeh starter (available from specialty stores)

Instructions:

1. Prepare the Beans: Rinse the soybeans thoroughly and soak them in water for 8–12 hours. Drain, rinse, and remove as much of the hulls as possible by gently rubbing the beans between your hands.
2. Cook the Beans: Boil the soybeans for 30 minutes, then drain and allow them to cool to about 90–95°F (warm but not hot to the touch).
3. Add the Starter: Once cooled, mix the soybeans with vinegar and sprinkle the tempeh starter evenly, stirring to coat.
4. Pack the Beans: Transfer the beans into a perforated plastic bag or a baking dish lined with banana leaves. Flatten the mixture to about 1–1.5 inches thick for even fermentation.
5. Ferment: Place the tempeh in an incubator or a warm spot (around 85–90°F) for 24–48 hours. White mold

will spread over the surface, binding the beans together when ready.
6. Store: Refrigerate the finished tempeh or slice and freeze for longer storage.

Tips:

- A constant temperature is key. Use a cooler wrapped with a light bulb for a makeshift incubator.
- Experiment with chickpeas or black beans for different flavors.
- If the mold smells unpleasant or turns black, discard it and sanitize your equipment before trying again.

Conclusion

Thank you for making it to the end of this fermentation guide! Whether you've skimmed through or read every section, you've taken an incredible step toward discovering one of the most ancient and rewarding culinary practices. Fermentation is far more than just a way to preserve food—it's an art, a science, and a window into flavors you might not have imagined possible in your own kitchen.

By now, you know that fermentation is a world of creativity. It's about taking simple, everyday ingredients like cabbage, milk, or flour, and transforming them into something totally unique and nutritious. With just a little salt, patience, and the help of nature's microorganisms, you've learned how to create vibrant foods bursting with flavor and health benefits. The best part? You don't need fancy equipment or rare ingredients—just an open mind and a willingness to play around with the process.

This guide has equipped you with the know-how, but that's just the beginning. The real magic of fermentation happens when you roll up your sleeves, choose your ingredients, and try it out for yourself. Maybe you'll start small with a jar of crunchy pickles or tangy sauerkraut, or maybe you're ready to take on bubbling kombucha or a nurturing sourdough starter. Whatever you choose, each project is both a learning experience and a delicious reward.

Fermentation is as much about experimenting as it is about patience. Don't be afraid to try new flavors, tweak recipes, or make mistakes along the way. If your first batch doesn't turn out perfectly, that's okay! Every ferment teaches you something new, whether it's the importance of keeping things submerged or how temperature can change the tang of your final creation. The more you practice, the more confident you'll become, and soon, you'll discover your own rhythm and style.

Beyond the kitchen, fermentation connects you to a larger story. When you ferment, you're tapping into traditions rooted in cultures around the world, from bold Korean kimchi to airy Ethiopian injera. You're also inviting sustainability into your home—turning fresh produce, even scraps, into something valuable, flavorful, and long-lasting. It's a reminder to slow down, work with nature, and savor the process as much as the final results.

Most importantly, this is meant to be fun! Celebrate every bubble, tangy sip, and crunchy bite. Take pride in watching ordinary ingredients transform before your eyes. Whether you're finding joy in gut-healthy foods or in sharing a homemade jar of pickles with a friend, fermentation is a gift that keeps giving, one bite at a time.

You now have the tools to start your fermentation adventure, but the possibilities are endless. Keep exploring, keep experimenting, and trust the process. Before long, your shelves will be lined with colorful jars, and your confidence in the kitchen will be soaring. You've got this—the world of fermentation is yours to shape. Thank you for letting this guide be your starting point, and here's to many exciting, flavorful discoveries ahead!

FAQs

What is the difference between fermentation and food spoilage?

Fermentation is a controlled process where beneficial microorganisms break down sugars and carbohydrates, resulting in preserved, flavorful, and nutrient-rich foods. Spoilage, on the other hand, occurs when harmful bacteria or molds take over, leading to unpleasant smells, tastes, and potential health risks. The key difference lies in proper preparation and maintaining the right conditions for fermentation, such as temperature, salt levels, and cleanliness.

How do I know if my ferment is safe to eat?

A healthy ferment will smell tangy, sour, or pleasantly funky, and may bubble during the process. Signs of spoilage include foul odors, slimy textures, or brightly colored mold (such as pink, black, or green). If you notice these, it's best to discard the batch. White, powdery kahm yeast on the surface is harmless and can simply be skimmed off.

Do I need special equipment to start fermenting at home?

No, you can start fermenting with basic kitchen tools like glass jars, a mixing bowl, and a wooden spoon. Items like fermentation weights, airlock lids, and cheesecloth can enhance the process but are not essential for beginners. You can also use everyday items like cabbage leaves or small jars as substitutes for weights.

What type of salt should I use, and how much is necessary?

Use non-iodized salt like sea salt, kosher salt, or pickling salt to ensure the beneficial bacteria thrive. For vegetable ferments, the general rule is to use 2–3% salt by weight of the vegetables and water. Too little salt may lead to spoilage, while too much can slow down the fermentation process.

How long does fermentation take?

The fermentation time depends on the recipe, temperature, and personal taste preferences. For example, sauerkraut may take 1–3 weeks, kombucha 7–14 days, and yogurt 6–12 hours. Taste your ferment periodically to check when it reaches your desired tanginess or flavor.

Why do I need to "burp" my jars, and how often should I do it?

During fermentation, gases like carbon dioxide build up inside the jar. If you're using an airtight lid, burping (loosening the lid) daily allows these gases to escape and prevents pressure buildup that could cause the jar to crack. If you're using airlock lids, they automatically release gas, so no burping is needed.

What should I do if my brine level drops during fermentation?

If the brine evaporates or is absorbed by the ingredients, top it off with a fresh brine made by dissolving 1–1.5 teaspoons of salt in 1 cup of water. Keeping all ingredients submerged under the brine is crucial to prevent exposure to air, which can lead to mold or spoilage. Always check your ferment daily to ensure proper submersion.

References and Helpful Links

The Editors of Encyclopaedia Britannica. (2024, October 23). Fermentation | Definition, Process, & Facts. Encyclopedia Britannica. https://www.britannica.com/science/fermentation

Apd, D. C. (2023, July 13). What is fermentation? The lowdown on fermented foods. Healthline. https://www.healthline.com/nutrition/fermentation

15 Fermented foods for a healthy gut and overall health - Dr. Axe. (2024, December 4). Dr. Axe. https://draxe.com/nutrition/fermented-foods/

Baseadmin. (2024, March 6). Fermenting Vegetables: A Step-by-Step Guide! Explore Yeast. https://www.exploreyeast.com/recipes/fermenting-vegetables-a-step-by-step-guide/

Measures to prevent bags swelling due to fermentation – Prevention of food spoilage by yeast, lactic acid bacteria, etc. – | Food preservative | FREUND Knowledge Ocean. (n.d.). FREUND Corporation. https://www.freund.co.jp/english/knowledge/article/detail/202206081051 35.html

Kris Bordessa, National Geographic author. (2024, January 3). Fermented Foods Recipes: 50+ to get you started. Attainable Sustainable®. https://www.attainable-sustainable.net/ferment-vegetables/

Ghafari, L. (2024, January 9). Lacto-Fermentation: How to ferment fruits and vegetables. Urban Farm and Kitchen. https://urbanfarmandkitchen.com/lacto-fermentation-how-to-ferment-fruits-and-vegetables/

www.ingramcontent.com/pod-product-compliance
Lightning Source LLC
LaVergne TN
LVHW012031060526
838201LV00061B/4554